A Pirate Named Molly

56 Limericks For Kids

With A **Bonus** How-To-Write-A-Limerick Guide!

Written by Randy Imwalle

Illustrated by Katie Imwalle

To my B.Y.W. Lisa. *RJI*

AUTHOR'S ACKNOWLEDGMENTS

I would like to thank Lisa Imwalle and Erin Imwalle for their encouragement and editorial support, and Ben Imwalle for his technical support I would also like to thank Sam Imwalle for permission to include *Today Is November First* in this book.

ISBN-13: 978-1481003636
Tenkids Publishing Company
Columbus, Ohio, USA

There once was a pirate named Molly

She had a green parrot called Polly

The bird liked to eat

Old pickled pigs' feet

No crackers for Polly, by golly!

There once was a reindeer named Charley

He loved to eat oats and barley

He said with a sigh,

"I'm too big to fly."

As he scooted around on his Harley.

There was a young angel named Sue
To the loftiest pine tree shc flew
When she got to the top
She decided to stop –
She had the most fabulous view.

There once was an elf named Harriet
She gathered the deer with her lariat
When she rounded up eight
She lined them up straight
And hooked them to Santa's chariot.

There once was a reindeer named Joe
But he'd one little problem you know
He said there's no way
He could pull Santa's sleigh
He was deathly afraid of the snow!

A leprechaun by the name of McNaught

Never before had been caught

He gave wishes three

So he'd be set free

To count all the gold in his pot.

From this house to that house I go
In the sun, and the rain, and the snow
Going left, going right
Always outside at night
My name you should certainly know.

There once was a groundhog named Phil
He liked to keep out of the chill
On Feb. 2 he saw
His shadow grown tall
So he scurried back under the hill.

There was a young turkey named Cletus
Told his mom, "I'm happy they feed us
But on Thanksgiving Day
Their prayers they'll pray
Then they'll sit at the table and eat us."

There once was a skeleton named Lance

And he really did like to dance

But Lance was dejected

His neighbors objected

'Cause he never did wear any pants!

There once was a pumpkin named Pat
On the covered front porch he sat
He started to wobble
Shake, shiver and bobble
And then that poor Pat went splat.

There once was a ghost called Blue Mary
Her problem – she wasn't too scary
Try as she might
She never caused fright
She looked like a big ripe Boo Berry!

Today is November first
My belly is ready to burst
Too much candy
Is a whack in the fanny
My belly is now truly cursed.

There once was an elf named Gertrude

She had a big problem with her ‘tude

So Santa did say

She must go away

Until she corrected her mood.

There is a young elf named Izzy
He says making toys makes him dizzy
So he sits on his bed
And eats stale bread
He's not a good helper now, is he?

I hope that your Christmas is merry
And your jolly St. Nick is hairy
But remember the reason
For this joyous season
Is Jesus, and Joseph, and Mary.

The snowstorm is starting to blow
The snowdrifts are starting to grow
They'll be little sorrow
With no school tomorrow
When snowballs kids happily throw.

By the light of an orange full moon

A skeleton plays an old tune

The witches and cats

And goblins and bats

Know that Halloween'll be here quite soon.

I see that spring is springing
The bee, its sting, is stinging
The grass now grows
The wind always blows
And the bird, its song, is singing.

Just listen to all us kids cheer
Summer is finally here
Free to play, free to run
Free to do what is fun
It's our favorite time of the year!

Scrunchy, scrunchy, scrunch
The leaves come down in a bunch
Red, yellow, and brown
They keep falling down
Let's pile them up after lunch!

There once was a creepy old witch

The thought of her near made me twitch

But she had a nice twin

With a similar grin

My thought? Which witch was which?

There was an old owl from Stoke
He listened much more than he spoke
The things that he heard
Made him quite a wise bird
As he sat on his perch in the oak.

There once was a chicken named Scat
He ate all the corn and got fat
So the good farmer's wife
Did sharpen her knife
And that was the end of poor Scat.

Was it a duck or a goose?
Whatever it was, it was loose
The children gave chase
But they couldn't keep pace
And their shouts and their screams were no use.

There once was a boy named Cole

He mailed his list to the Pole

But he fought with his brother

And lied to his mother

So Santa just gave him some coal.

There once was a reindeer named Brian
He was found in the barn loudly cryin'
When asked why so sad
He replied that he had
A logical fear of flyin'!

There was a shy, quiet boy named Jay
His voice remained silent all day
He took paper and pen
And wrote it down when
He ever had something to say.

There once was a boy from Hong Kong
He just loved to play a long song
But the crowd was dismayed
At the way that he played
When he missed and hit the wrong gong.

There was a young frog on a lily pad

Sometimes that frog was rilly bad

He jumped in the air'n

Was grabbed by a heron

And now that young frog is rilly sad.

There once was a spider named Matt
Who never did look where he sat
He hopped on the tuffet
Of Little Miss Muffet
And soon that poor spider was flat.

She wore a long cloak of red
As she delivered her grandma some bread
When she saw the big snout
She should have run out
That wasn't her grandma in bed!

Fritz was a small green iguana
He loved to lounge in the sauna
When his mom shouted, "Out!"
He started to pout
And whined, "But Ma, I don't wanna!"

Young Jeannie could not fall asleep
So her mom said to try counting sheep
She fell asleep when
She got just past ten
And her mom did not then hear a peep.

Nod, and Wynken, and Blynken
Set sail in a shoe without thinkin'
Then Mom sings a song
Not too short or too long
And baby, to slumber, is sinkin'.

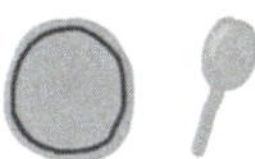

Answer for me this short riddle
Stop laughing, there's no time to diddle
Why'd the cow and the moon
And the dish and the spoon
Hang around with the cat and the fiddle?

The troll on the bridge was tough
And he hated the billy goats Gruff
The last goat of the three
Was stronger than he
And knocked the old troll on his duff.

There once was a Bigfoot named Larry

He certainly was very hairy

But the poor fellow

Had fur that was yellow

And he looked like a giant canary!

There once was a naughty young shepherd
Every day, for fun, he yelled, "Leopard!"
Soon all the good folk
Thought his scream was a joke
And the cat ate him up, salt and peppered!

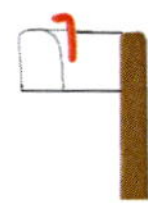

There once was a mailbox in Maine
It just stood in the sun and the rain
But put letters in it
And in just a minute
They're on their way over to Spain.

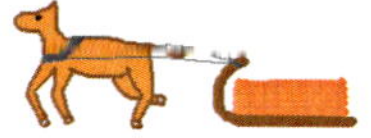

Two horses named Doc and Flory
Had a chance to go for the glory
They did their horsey best
And out pulled the rest
And that is the end of this story.

Hickory, dickory, dock

Two mice ran up the clock

The clock struck one

And she was done

Hickory, dickory, dock.

The wolf cried, "Little pig, let me in!"
"Never," said the pig, "By my chin!"
House of straw, house of sticks
The last, made of bricks
The wolf just couldn't get in.

Down the chimney, the wolf tried to squeeze
And he did come down like the breeze
But he fell in a pot
That was boiling hot
And the pigs, after that, lived with ease.

Old Toby was a day-dreaming beagle
Who thought he could fly like an eagle
While Toby's mind wandered
The other dogs pondered
Is a dream like that even legal?

Kip likes to sit and imagine

That his dog is really a dragon

Flaming breath is a threat

But what most makes him sweat

Is when Fido's tail starts a waggin'.

There once was a man named Sam
Whose favorite food was ham
But he ate it all up
And then had to sup
On a pretzel, some toast, and a yam.

A young witch lived close to the ocean
She searched for just the right potion
No newt eye or frog toes
No bat wool or dog nose
What she needed was high SPF lotion.

Listen to me – and I quote
There's one urgent need for a boat
Neither engine nor sail
Will cause it to fail
But you better make sure it will float!

Our Mary, she had a white lamb

It loved to eat toast and jam

But the lamb broke a rule

When it went to the school

So Ma'am told the lamb to scram.

The fox saw some grapes on the vine
"I'm hungry," he said, "So they're mine."
But the grapes were too high
And the fox couldn't fly
"They're sour, I'm sure," he did whine.

Brothers Orville and Wilbur Wright
Discovered the secret of flight
Getting up in the air, provoked not a scare
'Twas the landing that caused them the fright.

Though he couldn't explain just why
George Washington could not tell a lie
When he chopped down the tree
He said, "It was me."
That's the end of this tale, goodbye.

There once was a king in old France

He wore purple corduroy pants

He knew that his knickers

Caused lots of snickers

But he thought that they helped him to dance.

There was an old teacher at skool
She made her kids mind every rool
When she spanked a poor child
Who'd been a bit wild
They reckoned her terribly krool.

Twin brothers named Jim and Fizz Ed
Each wore a black goose on his head
When asked by Ms. Hoff
To take the birds off
They laughed, they turned, and they fled.

Said the cowboy, "Last night they attacked us
For days now, the bad guys have tracked us."
But truth be told, they weren't after his gold
Our hero, he sat on a cactus!

Bonus How-To-Write-A-Limerick Guide

Limericks have five lines. The first, second, and fifth lines rhyme with each other. The third and fourth lines rhyme with each other. This rhyme pattern is AABBA.

Limericks also have a distinct rhythm. The first, second, and fifth lines have three beats. The third and fourth lines have two beats.

We can use a classic limerick by Edward Lear to demonstrate. The **bold** syllables get the stress.

There **was** an old **man** in a **boat**
Who **said**, "I'm a**float**, I'm a**float**."
When they **said**, "No you **ain't**."
He was **rea**dy to **faint**
That un**hap**py old **man** in a **boat**

Pick the name of a person or place for the last word of the first line. Don't be bashful, you can start with your own name. We will use Nick. Make a list of rhyming words. If you need help use the Rhyming Word Cheat Sheet on the next page. Nick rhymes with brick, click, lick, quick, sick, slick, and trick and many other words.

There was a young boy named Nick
He thought he was pretty darn quick

The next two lines rhyme with each other. They also set up the scene or action for the last line.

He started the race
With a smirk on his face

The last line rhymes with the first two lines. It is usually funny, or has an unexpected twist.

But he cried when he tripped on a brick!

Rhyming Word Cheat Sheet

If the word you need rhymed starts with a vowel, add a letter from the list to your word. If the word you need rhymed starts with a consonant, replace the consonant with a letter from the list. I guarantee this Cheat Sheet will help you – unless your word is orange – then you are on your own!

A
B
BL
BR
C
CH
CL
CR
D
DR
DW
E
F
FL
FR
G
GH
GL
GR
H
I
J
K
KN
L
M
N
O
P
PL
PR

QU
R
S
SC
SCR
SH
SHR
SK
SL
SM
SN
SP
SPL
SPR
SQU
ST
STR
SW
T
TH
THR
TR
TW
U
V
W
WH
X
Y
Z

ABOUT THE AUTHOR

This is Randy's first book of limericks. He and his wife Lisa have ten children, and a beagle named Maggie. He would like to know what you think of this book. You can email him at RandyImwalle@att.net, or check out the **A Pirate Named Molly** Facebook page.

Made in the USA
Middletown, DE
16 December 2017